Name _____

Nicknames _____

Date of Birth or Adoption _____

Date of Passing _____

My earliest memories of finding you and bringing you home:

What you looked, felt and smelled like:

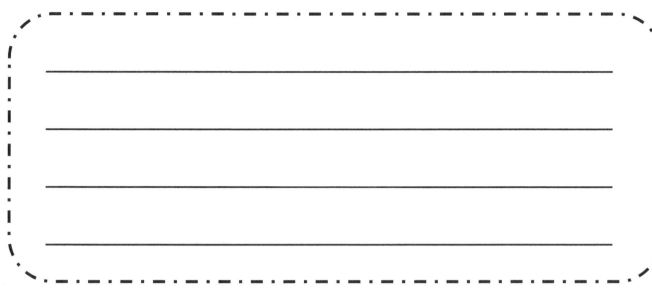

How you got your name:

Funny things you did while growing up:

Your personality traits:

Your funny and endearing habits:

Your favorite games, toys and foods:

The Top 10 reasons why I loved you:

Special times I remember:

Your final days:

How your declining health made me feel:

Why I will never forget you:

How you would want me to move forward:

My farewell letter to you:

Tributes from friends:

Made in United States
North Haven, CT
08 July 2023

38709478R00030